ORLI KOSHET

Between the Cracks of My Sanity

For Mikey, Milan, Ari, and Capri—
You are the light that fills all my cracks with gold.

No Mud, No Lotus

– Thich Nhat Hanh

Contents

Introduction

Introduction: Between the Cracks

Don't trust me. I sure as shit wouldn't.

I mean it. I'm not the authority here. I don't have the answers. I couldn't tell you how many times I've repeated the phrase "the more I learn the less I know" — and I've spent way to many years obsessing over learning.

For starters, I have been told that I am fickle, evasive, and incredibly indecisive. And though all those things are true, I'd love to provide you a little insight as to how I came to be this way. Most of it stems from the notion that I don't believe in one truth. I believe truth is subjective — and heavily shaped by your experience, your history, your specific version of the chaos. My experience is a tiny, unrecognizable grain of sand on a beachful of sand. It doesn't make it less real. It just means it's mine. Not yours. Therefore, how can lil ol' me claim to be all knowing if I am but a grain?!

So don't come here looking for answers. There aren't any. Not from me. Not from anyone.

What I can offer you is this:

An itty-bitty tiny grain of sand. An honest one.

I didn't write this book because I have it all figured out. I DO NOT have it figured out.

I wrote it because motherhood is the most chaotic and loneliest process I have ever been through.

Three times over.

I wrote it because I spent years feeling like I was the only one who couldn't find the balance, couldn't maintain the patience, couldn't locate herself underneath all the noise and the need and the never-ending list of things that only she could see needed doing.

I wrote it because I kept waiting for someone to say the true thing out loud. Not the Instagram version. Not the gratitude journal version. The real version. The 4:42 pm version. The airplane floor version. The front seat of the car in the dark version.

And when nobody said it — I decided to.

There's a version of me that lives at Bass Lake.

She's up before everyone else. The house is still. The morning has this specific kind of energy that belongs only to the hour before anyone needs anything — birds doing their thing, animals moving through the trees, the world already awake but not yet loud.

She's standing on a wooden porch, leaning on the railing, breathing cool air that hasn't been touched yet by the day. Waiting for the sun to warm her. Not rushing it. Just waiting.

That's who I'm always chasing.

Not a better mother. Not a published author. Not a thinner, more organized, more evolved version of myself (would be nice though).

Just that woman on the porch in the quiet that isn't silent. She is present. Unhurried. Temporarily relieved of the weight of everyone else's needs.

This book is the chase. Every chapter is a step toward that porch.

Not because I've arrived there permanently. But because I've learned — slowly, imperfectly, and mostly the hard way — how to find my way back to her.

And I think you have a version of her too.

Somewhere. Waiting.

This book is for her.

I

Part I: Cracking

The quiet unraveling

1

Chapter 1: 's Mom, Orli's Mom

And other casual identity crises

"I never know what to say when people ask what my hobbies are.
I mean, I am a MOM. I enjoy trips to the bathroom alone and
silence." #Truth

Y ou know those moments where you're watching everything unfold in slow motion, and even though you know what's about to happen ... you still can't stop it?
Yeah. This was kind of like that.

Move-in day at the University of Arizona. I was 17—nervcited (nervous and excited). The big day was finally here, and I was so ready to embrace all this newfound independence. My parents were there, being overbearingly helpful. My mom was in "high performance mode," efficiently organizing anything within reach.

We'd just finished wrestling a twin XL mattress into place when someone knocked at the door. It was another mom and her daughter, all bright smiles and well-rehearsed introductions. As they finished introducing themselves, my mom cheerfully beamed:

"Hi, I'm Orli."

And like an over-possessive name guard with zero chill, I immediately blurted:

"No, you're not. I'm Orli."

Cue the silence.

Some strange sideways glances. The longest pause ever.

My poor mother blinked and recovered.

"…'s mom. I'm Orli's mom."

Our guests nodded slowly—in that polite, we're-not-sure-what's-going-on-here-but-okay kind of way. They glanced between us with concern, as if unsure whether we were quirky or mid-breakdown.

Seventeen-year-old me was embarrassed and annoyed.

But it wasn't until I became a mother that the absurdity—and the truth—of that moment hit me full force.

The erasure.

The quiet disappearance of self.

The way you become someone's adjunct—a "plus one" to your child's name—while the person you once were gets left somewhere between fluorescent-lit hallways and overstuffed Target bins.

No one warns you about that.

Let's get this straight:

Motherhood is not a rebranding.

It's not a cute little identity tweak.

It's a metaphysical identity demolition—followed by years of reconstruction—while you simultaneously wipe asses, find missing shoes, and negotiate with Polly Pocket–sized ninjas over the color of their sippy cup.

And that's just the toddler years.

"They say you'll never be the same after kids."

Thanks for the vague foreshadowing.

What they should say is: "Welcome to insanity. You are about to become twelve versions of yourself—some who lose it over spilled breast milk, and others who lose it in the middle of a parking lot over who sassed who first—all while praying for a five-minute break in your new home office: the bathroom."

There's actually a name for what happens to your identity when you become a mother.

Researchers call it *fracturing*.

Not breaking—fracturing.

The distinction matters.

A fracture means the original structure is still there, just reorganized under pressure.

Which is exactly what it feels like.

You're not gone.

You're just rearranged in ways nobody warned you about.

The "Orli's Mom" moment wasn't just a social hiccup.

It was a preview.

A prelude to the psychic split that happens when identity collides with motherhood.

There's who you were (BK—before kids).

There's who you become to raise them.

There's the insane standard you hold yourself to.

And then there's the quiet, invisible work of trying to stitch all those pieces together—without completely losing yourself.

I know this work intimately.

The first time I was promoted to "mom" was a monumental experience — not just because I created a human, but because I successfully kept her alive while losing every ounce of myself in the process. Somewhere around month three, I finally managed to locate this "self" I had misplaced. Truth be told, I didn't even know she was gone. I was literally just surviving — exhausted, drained, burnt out, and lonely — but still somehow, miraculously, doing it. Between the baby cuteness overload, warm snuggles, toothless smiles, and soul-filling giggles, I couldn't deny that I was still super depleted.

It took a couple of months to upgrade to my badass "new-mom" self, but once I did, I felt pretty unstoppable. I did this whole song and dance three times, and I gotta tell you — sometimes it still feels just as hard as that first time.

No one can ever truly prepare anyone for the unfathomable loss of self and the subsequent reconstruction of identity that happens when you become a mother. It's the most complicated and tremendous transition any woman who takes on this role will ever face. Each child's arrival is like a rebirth. The kicker? Just when you think you've got it down because you've done it before, your world gets violently shaken all over again, and you're left waiting for the snow to settle in your glitter globe.

Everyone's experiences are different. For me, the biggest phase of self-reconstruction came with becoming a mother for the first time. But the rediscovery of self between kid #2 and #3? That was a whole other beast. My first two are 15 months apart — which meant that while I was dealing with teething, sleep deprivation, endless unsolicited opinions on breastfeeding vs. formula, and constantly on tiny toy pick-up patrol, my storm never really had a chance to settle.

Once your older kids start school and you realize you're getting some of yourself back, it can feel like an unexpected ice bucket challenge — one minute you're getting a breather, and the next, it's all gone again.

So how do we make this process a little less shitty?

We start by stopping to pretend the cracks aren't there.

Because here's what nobody tells you about falling apart — the cracks are exactly where the light gets in.

Let's find the light

Activity: Just Start Somewhere

I could give you a list of twenty questions. But you can find that in other books — and honestly, it doesn't feel authentic to me.

So here's what you can do if you feel like it:

Grab your phone, a notebook, the back of a receipt — whatever's closest. And just answer these. Quickly. Before your inner critic shows up with her opinions.

What's your guilty pleasure? The one you judge yourself for the second you admit it. Write it down. Verbalize it to yourself, think it ... doesn't matter just make notice of it. Extra points if it's embarrassing.

When was the last time you felt like yourself — not a mom, not a partner, not someone's everything — just you? Where were you? What were you doing?

If you had three child-free hours and nobody would ever know how you spent them — what would you actually do?

Don't overthink it. The first answer is usually the truest one.

2

Chapter 2: Juggling the Fuck Out of Overwhelm

"I always thought I would be a patient mom, and then I watched my son try to zip his own jacket." #InhaleExhale

I remember standing in the shower—eyes closed, hot water running, finally alone for approximately four minutes—and being completely convinced my baby was dying. She wasn't crying. There was no sound. Just silence.

Which was somehow worse.

My brain, now apparently rewired for catastrophe, filled the silence immediately.

What if she put the blanket over her face?

What if she scratched her cornea with those tiny, impossible-to-cut, sharp-ass baby nails?

What if—somehow, at one month old—she was a prodigy who figured out how to crawl, climb onto the bed, and roll off to her impending doom? None of it was likely.

All of it felt real.

I rinsed my hair in approximately eleven seconds and ran out of the bathroom—soaking wet, heart racing—to find her exactly where I left her.
Fine. Completely fine.
Staring at the ceiling like the tiny existential philosopher she was.
That was my introduction to momxiety.
Not the sleepless nights.
Not the feeding schedule.
The shower.

The four minutes I tried to take for myself and couldn't—because even when my body was alone, my brain never was. That was eleven years ago.

My kids are now 12, 11, and 5. The blanket-over-the-face fear is gone. But momxiety? She didn't leave. She just got a wardrobe change.

Now morning momxiety sounds like this:
Did the middle get his medication this morning?
Did he wash his face before sticking contacts in (didn't we go over this already)?
Are the oldest shorts covering her cherished goods?
WTF is up with these stupid bathing suit tan lines, and why is she drawing freckles on her face? What even is that trend?
What am I making everyone for breakfast? for lunch? and dinner?
Where are the water bottles?
Did I already feed the dang cat?
Where the effff is my coffee?!

Same anxiety. Different phases.

Same brain that never fully turned off.

That is momxiety.

Not a clinical term.

Not a phase you grow out of.

Just the permanent background hum of a mother's mind—constantly scanning, constantly anticipating, constantly carrying what nobody else is carrying.

It's not just what you do.

It's what you carry.

And it is overwhelming.

Motherhood is an unconquerable hamster wheel. You think this task will be the one that lets you breathe—and then another one shows up. And another. And another.

There's no finish line.

Ever.

We keep running, hoping the next thing will give us a second to catch our breath.

But it doesn't.

We just keep spinning.

Or, as Dory so eloquently put it—just keep swimming.

Never mind that, anyway you slice it, we are primarily responsible for the health and wellness of our children. With each new child, our plate of responsibility grows—and somehow there's still no room for dessert.

Which feels deeply unfair, because I, for one, am a sucker for chocolate.

Yes, it may have taken two of you to make the baby, but make no mistake—unless you have a wildly progressive, unicorn-level balanced household (and good on you!)—that child's wellness and ability to thrive funnels mostly through you.

You are the default.

Which means the questions come to you.

The decisions come to you.

The worries live with you.

Everything from fevers to friendships, heartbreak to homework, food choices to safety, social media to self-esteem—you are the central processing unit for all of it.

It is a lot.

It is overwhelming.

For me, one of the hardest parts of this phase was the quiet resentment—sometimes not so quiet—toward my partner, who didn't seem to have his entire identity and daily functioning flipped upside down by any of this.

And that's real too.

What helps

You don't outrun overwhelm.

You don't push through it.

You stop—for a second, even when stopping feels impossible—and name what's actually happening.

Not "I'm fine."

Not "I'm just tired."

The real thing.

Frustration.

Guilt.

Resentment.

Exhaustion.

All of it. Without judging yourself for feeling it.

Because sometimes it's not one big thing.

It's seventy-three small things that have been quietly stacking up all week. Emotional clutter is real. And it's heavy.

And the only way to start moving it is to notice it's there.

Then ask yourself one question:

Not *what should I do?*

Not *what would a good mom do?*

Just—

What do I need right now?

It won't feel like this forever.

The only constant in life is change.

Activity

Just one question. Sit with it honestly.

Where can you find help—and what can you outsource?

Not theoretically.

Actually.

This week. In your real life.

Maybe it's asking your partner to handle one thing without being asked twice.

Maybe it's a family member.

A friend.

A paid hour of help.

Maybe it's lowering a standard you've been white-knuckling for no reason.

You don't have to do all of it alone.

You were never supposed to.

And if asking for help feels uncomfortable—good.

That means it's working.

The DBC Method

Delegate. Be Specific. Compliment.
Don't hint.
Don't assume.
Don't seethe quietly while doing everything yourself.
Ask clearly.
Say exactly what you need.
Then reinforce it.
As the saying goes—you catch more bees with honey than vinegar.
For those who've read *Why Men Marry Bitches*—be the dumb fox.
For the rest of you, go read it.

The concept is simple: develop the skill set of making your partner feel like their help is the most incredible, significant contribution anyone has ever made to your household.

Here's a real example:
Your partner is supposed to take out the trash.
What you want to say:
"Can you take the trash out?"
"You still haven't taken the trash out."
"Why do I have to do everything around here?!"

What actually works:
"You're so great at helping with the trash—I really appreciate it."
"You're so strong and this bag is heavy for me—can you grab it?"

Try not to say it dripping in sarcasm. We're going for effectiveness here.
If someone feels appreciated, they're far more likely to help again.
That's not manipulation.
That's just how humans work.

And if you're doing this solo—think about where else support can come from.

Family.

Friends.

Paid help.

Swapping childcare.

Even small pockets of breathing room.

Asking for help doesn't make you weak.

It makes you resourceful.

It makes you less resentful.

And low-key—it makes you intelligent AF.

Bonus: The DBC method isn't just for other people. It works for you too.

Acknowledge your effort.

Be specific about what you actually accomplished today.

Give yourself credit—even for the small things.

Because those small things? They're not small at all.

3

Chapter 3: The Witching Hour (4:42 p.m.)

A chapter about noise, motherhood, and why my nervous system needs an exorcism

"'Tis now the very witching time of night, when hell itself breathes contagion into the world." — *William Shakespeare,* Hamlet

Clearly, he was never a mother at 4:42 pm.

The first time I heard the term *witching hour* I was stuffed into a van with my sister-in-law, her kiddos, my parents, and what felt like the entire contents of a Target baby aisle.

We were out of the country, all driving together somewhere - and to be honest the details of where we were going are genuinely vague. What I do remember is this: my eldest was about a year old, it was mid-afternoon, and she suddenly - without warning or apparent cause - completely went batshit bonkers. Now, she was a fairly chill baby. As long as she was right beside me at every given moment, she was chill. So this? This was a weird moment.

I did everything. We pulled the van over, I fed her, changed her, burped her, rocked her. Made the shushing sound repeatedly. Checked for rogue sock seams, offered every object within arm's reach as a potential source of comfort.

Nothing.

And the drive wasn't even all that far... we were so close.

She was just... inconsolable. Furious at the universe. A tiny, beautiful, completely irrational rage machine strapped into a car seat.

And then my sister-in-law — veteran mother (of five)— turned, looked over at my baby, looked at me, and shrugged with the calm, knowing, non-judgmental energy of someone who has been to war and come back whole.

"Must be witching hour."

Just like that.

I had no idea what she meant. But I felt instantly less insane.

Snapple fact: Did you know that the term witching hour traces back to Shakespeare — that moment in Hamlet where darkness takes over and hell itself breathes contagion into the world. He meant midnight. He meant witches and demons and supernatural chaos.

But somewhere between 1600 and now, mothers claimed it. Because if Shakespeare needed a word for the hour when everything inexplicably falls apart — we needed it more.

For babies, it's that fussy, inconsolable late afternoon window that arrives like clockwork and leaves just as mysteriously. For mothers of older kids, it just... evolves. The chaos changes shape but the hour remains sacred.

My sister-in-law knew. She's lived it five times over.

And at 4:42 p.m., I still hear her voice.

Must be witching hour.

If motherhood were a horror movie, the jump-scare wouldn't happen at midnight.

It happens at 4:42 pm.

The air in my house doesn't smell like lavender or fresh linen at this hour. It smells like the 22nd mile of a 30k marathon — a stale cocktail of exhaustion, chaos, and possibly burnt chicken. The "Atomic" systems of the morning have officially disintegrated, vanished, and evaporated. Whatever version of me showed up at 7 am with her lists and her intentions? She has left the building.

The 4:42 Archetypes

Every household has them. Mine looks like this:

The littlest — desperately in need of a bath, entertainment, and has secretly consumed more chocolate than the children at Charlie's factory. She is hangry, sticky, dirty, and staring at me with the existential dread of a Victorian orphan.

The middle — stuck in homework purgatory for way too long, officially rocking the one-sock look, fingers desperately twitching for his phone, having read the same social studies article ten times without absorbing a single word.

The eldest — panic-texting between dance classes to make sure she hasn't been forgotten at the studio. Forwarding five reminder emails from school, and announcing she is starved and in desperate need of a real dinner.

Me — the alter ego is threatening to surface. The one who needs coffee, two minutes of silence, and some basic reassurance that she is still a functional human being and not just a meal-producing, chaos-managing, emotionally-available-on-demand appliance.

The Nervous System Exorcism

I know exactly what's happening. This is sensory overload. My nervous system isn't just stressed — it needs a literal exorcism.

Why does my middlest choose this specific moment to take up beatboxing while rocking back and forth on his chair? Why does the oven timer create a frequency that makes my skin feel two sizes too small? Why does my littlest need to tell me — on repeat, with full narrative detail — the story about how someone pushed her during lineup?

I know why. Because they're kids. Because this is 4:42. Because this is just what it is.

But knowing that doesn't stop the mombie from rising.

The mombie is what happens when the patient, present, emotionally-regulated mother I genuinely try to be runs out of bandwidth. She doesn't disappear dramatically. She just... surfaces. Slowly. With dead eyes and a coffee cup she's reheated four times.

When I feel her coming I do the only responsible thing available to me.

I look at my middlest and I say, with complete sincerity:

"I need a ten minute coffee break or I am about to go full mombie on everyone."

He nods. He understands. We have been here before.

And then I turn on Avatar for the littlest.

Not because I'm failing. Not because I've given up. But because Avatar is her all time most favorite movie and it buys me ten minutes of lineup-story silence, and ten minutes is enough to reheat my coffee, breathe like a human, eat mini Trader Joes knock-off snickers without sharing, and return to the kitchen as something closer to a mother than a mombie.

The thing nobody tells you about the witching hour

It's not a character flaw. It's not proof you're doing it wrong.

It's sensory overload — and the fact that you can feel it coming before you snap? That's not nothing. That's everything. Most mothers don't catch it until they're already in it, already said the thing they didn't mean, already feeling the guilt settling in like a second shift.

Learning to recognize your specific trigger — before it triggers you — is the whole game.

For me it's noise. Too much of it, all at once, from every direction. The audible kind, the visual kind, the mental kind. It becomes one unbearable frequency and my nervous system starts screaming for an exit.

Maybe for you it's being touched too much. Or too many questions. Or the weight of seventeen things unfinished. Whatever it is — *know your thing.* Because you can't turn down the volume on something you haven't named yet.

Activity: The Witching Hour Toolkit

This one isn't for journaling. Stick it on your fridge if you have to.

In the moment — when it hits:

Step 1: Name the trigger. What is it right now? Noise? Touch? Mental load? Just name it. Out loud if you have to. *"This is sensory overload. I know what this is."* Naming it stops the spiral before it starts.

Step 2: Silence what you can — without guilt. One screen. One room. Whatever buys you ten minutes of reduced input. You are not failing. You are regulating.

Step 3: Take care of the most basic physical need first. Water. Coffee. Three deep breaths. One minute outside. Go pee. Your nervous system cannot problem-solve when it's running on empty.

Step 4: Reintroduce slowly. Not all at once. Start with one child, one conversation, one task. The middle and his homework first. One on one. Calm before the chaos resumes.

After the storm — two questions for later:

When the kids are in bed and you have two quiet minutes:

1. What was my trigger today — and did I catch it before or after I snapped? No judgment. Just notice.
2. What's one thing I could do tomorrow to lower the volume *before* 4:42 hits?

4

Chapter 4: I Can't Play Barbies, But I'll DIY You a Barbie Closet

"Some days, it feels a little bit more like negotiating with a band of drunken, bipolar pirates than actual parenting."
#PiratesOfSanity

I hate playing.

There. I said it.

Not playing with my kids specifically. Just playing in general. The Barbies with no narrative arc.

The made-up games with rules that change every thirty seconds, and somehow I'm always losing.

The pretend scenarios that require me to be a specific character with a specific voice—and God forbid I get it wrong.

I love my kids a whole lot.

And I hate playing.

For years, I felt guilty about that. Like there was something fundamentally wrong with me as a mother because I couldn't lose myself in a game of pretend for forty-five minutes without checking how much time had passed.

But here's what I figured out somewhere between the volleyball tournaments, the basketball games, the homework, and the hygiene standards that are—let's be honest—met only somewhat:

I enjoy my kids the most when I'm actually having fun too.

Not their version of fun.

Mine.

By the end of a full week, I am T-O-A-S-T.

Tired.

Overwhelmed.

Annoyed.

Stressed.

Tense.

And a **TOAST**ed mother who is forcing herself to play Barbies with zero enthusiasm is not connecting with her kids.

She's performing.

And everyone in the room can feel the difference.

So I decided to stop performing.

And I started finding my version of fun.

For me, it's bubbles.

It's evening walks where my kids pick every flower they see (my neighbors slightly hate us), and I let them (within reason).

It's dandelions—every single one we pass, we stop, we make a wish, we blow.

Then I ask what they wished for.

Sometimes they tell me.

Sometimes they don't.

The wishing isn't really the point.

None of that is playing.

All of it is connecting.

And I've slowly come to understand that there's a profound difference between the two.

Playing requires you to enter their world on their terms and perform with enthusiasm you don't always have.

Connection just requires you to be next to each other in a moment that feels real.

Present.

Unhurried.

Yours. Theirs.

The bubbles cost less than two dollars.

The dandelions are free.

The walks take twenty minutes—and somehow reset everything.

You don't have to be the mom who gets on the floor and plays for hours.

You just have to find your version of showing up.

These battery-draining leprechauns look to you for everything—and yes, I mean everything.

So you have to find a charging station.

Something that fills you while you're with them.

Something that makes the endless daily drudgery a little lighter.

Match their outfits if that's your thing.

Do the sunset stroll.

Play the stupid TikTok dance in the kitchen.

Listen to your podcast while you fold laundry together.

Find the thing that makes you feel like you **and** like their mom at the same time.

Get creative.

Get silly.

Adjust your expectations.

And stop making yourself play Barbies if you hate Barbies.

Shit, girl—build the Barbie closet if DIY is more your jam.

Activity

Just one question: What's your version of the dandelion?

Take a second and think of what you make yourself do that you strongly dislike doing—and then think about what you actually enjoy doing with your kids.

Find that thing.

Do it this week.

Even once.

That's enough.

5

Chapter 5: Please Make Sure You All Talk at Once

A chapter about noise, the car, and the emotional surround sound of motherhood

"Please, all of you – talk at once. It's my favorite way to process information" #SendHelp

There is a specific kind of chaos that happens between 2:45 and 3:30 p.m. that I don't think gets enough airtime.

Not the witching hour.

Not the morning scramble.

The pickup.

It starts with the littlest.

I know how this works, so I come prepared—a Kinder egg.

Not just any chocolate.

It has to be a Kinder egg.

Chocolate is currency in this operation, and the denomination matters.

She gets in, opens it, and tells me about her day in the way only a five-year-old can—which is mostly a detailed inventory of new bruises she has collected, along with a firm assessment of who was mean during lineup and who was sick and not in school today.

Five minutes later, I'm back in the school pickup line waiting for my son.

I've learned to read his body language before he even opens the door.

I can tell from his posture.

From the way he's walking.

From the set of his jaw.

If someone told him he wasn't good at whatever sport he played that day—it's going to be a long ride.

He gets in.

I ask how he is.

He tells me who said what, how it made him feel, how much homework he has, what's fair, and what isn't.

And I listen.

I hold it.

I don't react.

Mostly, I try to help him separate the moment from the whole day.

Because for a long time, every single day was the worst day of his entire life.

Wednesdays especially.

We started doing "suck, sweet, and act of kindness" early—second grade, maybe—but it wasn't until fourth grade that something shifted.

I started helping him see that it wasn't his whole day that was bad.

It was a moment.

One moment in time can be not awesome—but that's all it ever is.

One moment.

And a moment doesn't have to shadow everything that comes after it, or everything that came before it.

This year has been better.

Thank the holy heavens above.

Then it's off to middle school pickup we go.

I have approximately five minutes to get from her school to her dance studio.

She, unlike the others, doesn't offer information.

I have to ask the right questions or she shuts down completely.

I am predictable, so she almost always gives me the same BS answers—but we do the dance every day.

Who did you sit with at lunch?

How were the girls?

How much homework?

Test scores she volunteers freely.

Everything else requires excavation.

Three kids.

Three completely different emotional operating systems.

Twelve minutes total.

One moving vehicle.

And I'm supposed to hold space for all of it—listening, reframing, not reacting, staying present—while also driving and not hitting any of the e-bike kids who are now ascending like flies on an unattended BBQ.

The noise isn't just sound.

It's weight.

It's three separate worlds landing in your lap before you've had a single second to put down your own.

The thing about noise

The thing about noise

It's not just the volume.

It's the simultaneity. Everyone needing something at the exact same moment — your attention, your validation, your answers, your presence. All of it at once. All of it urgent. All of it real.

Researchers call it the mental load — the cognitive and emotional labor of anticipating, planning, and managing family life that lives almost entirely in one person's head. A 2024 study out of USC found that mothers perform 73% of all cognitive household labor. Not the dishes. Not the laundry. The thinking behind the dishes. The planning behind the laundry. The mental architecture that holds the whole thing up.

And here's what that study also found — this invisible thinking work was more unevenly distributed than the physical work. Meaning we've made progress on who does the dishes. We've made almost none on who carries the map.

The mental load doesn't clock out when the car pulls into the driveway. It doesn't pause for dinner. It doesn't sleep. Research shows it is boundaryless — unbound by time, space, or place. It percolates through the everyday. Through the pickup line and the homework table and the bedtime routine and the moment after everyone is finally asleep when you're still running through tomorrow's list in your head.

I don't know who to help first.

I never say that out loud. But it's there — every single afternoon — underneath the listening and the holding and the not reacting.

So I help all of them. Not perfectly. Not in the order they needed. But I show up for each one and I keep moving.

We get home. Hands get washed. Backpacks get opened. Homework gets reviewed at the same kitchen table where I'm also half-making dinner and half-listening to the littlest who has forgotten the Kinder egg and needs something else entirely.

The twelve minutes in the car just became three more hours.

The noise doesn't stop. It just changes rooms.

And you move with it. Every single day. Carrying more than anyone sees. Doing more than anyone counts.

That's not a bad mother.

That's just a mother.

Activity

You just carried a lot in that car.

Find something funny. A meme. A stupid video. A ridiculous story. Make light of something heavy in a way that feels safe.

Or just let them pick the music.

Seriously. I hand over my phone and let them search Spotify for whatever feels right.

Laughter and music don't fix the noise. But they change its frequency.

And sometimes that's enough to remind everyone — including you — that you're all on the same team.

II

PART II: Feeling

Anger, Tenderness, and Truth That Doesn't Always Fit

6

Chapter 6: What Even Is This Body? And Who's Been Using it Without My Permission

"To lose something, you first have to gain it."
#WhoAteAllTheFeelings

I turned 40, and I'm not super happy about it.

Not about wrinkles.

Not about the white hairs quietly staging a hostile takeover.

Not even the subtle but consistent betrayal of gravity across my body.

I can handle all of that.

What I can't shake—

is the handstand.

And the cartwheel.

Two things I couldn't do as a kid—but always assumed I'd eventually get around to. And now I'm realizing I might die in this body having never done either one.

That's a very specific kind of grief.

The kind no one talks about.

The kind that has nothing to do with how your body looks—and everything to do with what it never got to be.

And here's the part that's harder to admit:
This is just another fracture.
Not the kind where everything falls apart—
the kind where something shifts, and you don't get to go back.

My body didn't just change.
It did something extraordinary that I don't think I gave it nearly enough credit for.
It carried life. Three times. It expanded beyond what I thought was possible, was cut open and sutured back together, and kept going. It fed people from itself. It survived sleep deprivation that would qualify as a human rights violation in other contexts. It absorbed stress, held tension, and ran on coffee and determination for years.
And I spent most of that time criticizing it.
Of course it doesn't look the same as before.
How could it?
It isn't the same body. It's a body that has been through something. Several somethings. And bodies that go through things carry the evidence of having done so — not as failure, but as record.
Here's what I've had to make peace with:
I cannot go back to the high school version of myself. Not because I didn't try hard enough or want it badly enough. But because that version of me hadn't done any of this yet.
She was lighter — in every sense of the word. And I am not her anymore.
I've expanded. In ways that have nothing to do with weight.
So the work stopped being about getting back.
It became about showing up for the body that's actually here.

And that required a complete reframe — because somewhere along the way, without really noticing, my body stopped being something I lived in and became something I managed.

A project.

A problem.

Something to fix, tighten, shrink, or get back to some earlier version of.

Or — on the other end — something I was supposed to love unconditionally and effusively at all times, as if the relationship between a woman and her postpartum, post-surgery, sleep-deprived, stress-holding body is just one long soft-focus Instagram moment.

Those always felt like the only two options.

Fix it. Or perform loving it.

Neither one ever fit.

But what if there's a third option nobody talks about?

Not fixing it. Not performing love for it.

Just… living in it.

Not as a consolation prize. Not as giving up. But as a genuine, radical, deeply countercultural choice to stop evaluating your body long enough to actually inhabit it.

I don't love my body every day. I want to be honest about that because the alternative — pretending I've arrived at some enlightened state of unconditional body acceptance — would be a lie, and you'd feel it.

Some days I catch my reflection and think — okay, we're doing alright.

Some days I don't look.

Most days I just get on with it.

And lately, getting on with it feels like enough.

For a long time I thought the goal was to feel good about my body. To reach some finish line where I'd look in the mirror and genuinely like what I saw without immediately cataloging everything that needed fixing.

That finish line kept moving.

So I changed the goal.

Not feeling good about my body. Feeling at home in it.

And those are not the same thing.

Feeling good is conditional. It shifts with the number on the scale, the phase of your cycle, how much sleep you got, what you ate, whether the lighting in the dressing room was designed by someone who hates women. It's dependent on too many variables to be reliable.

Feeling at home is different.

It's quieter. Less performance, more patience. It doesn't require the mirror to cooperate. It just requires you to stop treating your body like a renovation project and start treating it like somewhere you actually live.

And what I've come to accept:

I don't fully understand my body. What it holds. Why it holds it. The honest answer is—it's complicated. Sometimes it's hormones. Sometimes it's genetics. Sometimes it's the girl dinner that turned into three glasses of wine and the best night of the month. Sometimes it's exhaustion so deep it rewires your appetite. Sometimes it's depression wearing a snack.

It's all of it. None of it. Something different every season.

And sometimes the body holds things until you're ready to look at them.

It comes back—not to punish you.

To finish the conversation.

And sometimes the conversation doesn't have a neat ending.

I've stopped needing it to.

Because feeling at home in your body doesn't require you to have solved it. It doesn't require the insight or the answer or the finished conversation.

It just requires you to stop waiting until you've figured it out before you're allowed to be here.

And now I'm here.

Forty.

Thinking about a handstand.

And realizing—it was never about the handstand.

It was about the assumption that I would come back to myself.

That I would eventually have the time.

The space.

The energy.

To try. To play. To move.

To be in my body—not just responsible for it.

Right now, I'm just noticing.

What I missed. What I ignored. What I postponed.

Not with judgment.

Just with awareness.

Because awareness feels like the first step back.

Back into a body that isn't just something to manage—but something to live in.

I'm not suddenly signing up for adult gymnastics classes or chasing some version of myself that existed twenty years ago (but if you're down email me and maybe we could do it together ;p)

That's not the point.

The point is noticing.

And maybe—slowly—finding my way back.

Not to who I was.
But to who I am now.

Because this body—the one I've been criticizing, ignoring, negotiating with—
has been doing its job the whole time.

It carried babies.
It survived sleepless nights. It held stress, tension, and more mental load than I can probably quantify.
It showed up.
Even when I didn't.

And maybe the goal isn't to fix it.
Or love it.
Or get it back.

Maybe the goal is just to stop treating it like something I need to manage.
To listen a little more. To notice a little sooner.
To move—not because I should, but because I can.

Maybe it's as small as:
Standing in the kitchen and stretching for no reason.
Walking a little slower.
Letting myself feel where I am instead of rushing past it.

Nothing dramatic.
Nothing performative.
Just... returning.

And I know with absolute certainty—

I'll be working on that handstand.

Not because I need to prove anything. Not because it means something about my body or my worth.

But just because - If I reach 50 and I still can't do any of this shit I'll be pretty annoyed I didn't even try.

Activity

What are you still trying to "get back to"?

And what would it look like to stop going backward—and just meet yourself where you are?

7

Chapter 7: Sacrifice ≠ Love

"You don't need to set yourself on fire to keep everyone else warm." #SacrificeIsNotLove

The word *sacrifice* comes from the Latin *sacrificium*—from *sacer*, meaning sacred, and *facere*, meaning to make.

To make sacred.

Not to deplete.

Not to give until there's nothing left.

Not to smile through the erasure and call it love.

To make something sacred.

Somewhere between ancient Rome and the children's section of Barnes & Noble, we lost that.

Most of us learned what maternal sacrifice looks like from a picture book.

You know the one.

A tree.

A boy.

A lifetime of taking.

The tree gives her apples, her branches, her trunk—until there is nothing left but a stump.

The boy sits on the stump.

The tree calls it happiness.

We were supposed to find that beautiful.

I find it unrealistic, depleting, incorrect, and outright terrifying.

Not because mothers shouldn't give.

But because what *The Giving Tree* describes isn't love.

It's erasure with a smile.

It's the slow dismantling of a whole person dressed up as devotion.

And we handed that book to our children and said—this.

This is what love looks like.

It isn't.

Love is not a transaction where one party gives until they disappear.

Love—real love, sustainable love, the kind that actually raises healthy humans—is an exchange.

Energy in.

Energy out.

Not always equal.

Not always perfectly balanced.

But moving in both directions.

And here's what nobody tells you about your children:

They are not taking from you.

They are teaching you.

These tiny, chaotic, occasionally maddening little humans are the most concentrated curriculum you will ever encounter.

Every impossible moment is a lesson.

Every boundary pushed is an invitation to know yourself better.

Every 4:42 pm. witching hour, every pickup, every difficult situation, every "today was the worst day of my life" Wednesday—

It feels like depletion.

And sometimes it is.

But underneath that, if you're paying attention, it is also expansion.

You are not the Giving Tree.

You are a student who also happens to be in charge.

The distinction matters.

Because the Giving Tree model—give everything, need nothing, call it happiness—doesn't just harm you.

It harms them.

Because children who grow up watching their mother disappear learn that love requires self-erasure.

That showing up for others means abandoning yourself.

That the measure of devotion is how much you're willing to lose.

That is not the lesson.

The lesson is this:

You can love fiercely and still have needs.

You can give generously and still have limits.

You can be fully present for your children and still be a whole person.

Actually—

You can only be fully present for your children **if** you are still a whole person.

And yes - I fully acknowledge I'm an asshole and might be the only person on earth who has issues with a beloved children's classic. I own two copies. I've read it to my kids more times than I can count. Shel Silverstein was clearly onto something about love and generosity that has moved generations of people to tears.

But these are my truths.
You have yours.
Disagree with me - that's the point.

Activity
Where in your life are you being the Giving Tree?

Not where you're giving—giving is good, giving is part of this.
But where are you giving in a way that is making you less, not more?

Where is the exchange broken—everything flowing one direction, nothing coming back?
Name it.
Just name it.

You don't have to fix it today. But you do have to see it.

8

Chapter 8: Anger Isn't a Parenting Fail

"My kids call it 'yelling' when I raise my voice. I call it motivational speaking for the selective listener." #AngryGumball

I tell my clients this all the time:
Anger is a gift.
Not a flaw.
Not a failure.
Not proof that you're doing it wrong or that you're too much or that you need to work on your patience.

A gift.

Anger is information.
It's your body's way of announcing—loudly, urgently, sometimes inconveniently—that a boundary has been crossed.

That the exchange has been broken.
That something needs attention that hasn't been getting it.

The problem isn't the anger.

The problem is that nobody taught us how to receive the gift.

The volcano

My anger starts at the bottom.

A slow heat that builds somewhere deep and rises—through the stomach, through the chest, up through the throat—until it reaches the top of my head and there is nowhere left for it to go.

And here's the thing about the moment it finally erupts:

It's never about the thing it's about.

Because the thing—the dumb noise, the stupid comment, the inconsequential moment that finally breaks the seal—that's just the last straw. The one small thing that lands on top of a pile that's been building for hours. Days. Weeks sometimes.

Here's what the volcano was actually made of:

The mental calculations that started before my feet hit the floor. The medication that needed to be given before school. The emotional triage of three different kids with three different needs in twelve minutes of car time. The invisible work of noticing everything that needs to be done and figuring out who will do it and when. The resentment that accumulates quietly, steadily, when you realize you've been managing everything—including everyone else's feelings—and you're still carrying your own personal bullshit that hasn't had a single minute of airtime.

None of that announced itself.

None of that got a moment to breathe.

It just stacked. Quietly. Completely. Until it didn't.

And then someone made a dumb noise.

And off the volcano went.

This isn't a character flaw. This is what happens when a nervous system absorbs more than it can metabolize. Research on stress physiology shows that unprocessed emotional load doesn't disappear— it accumulates in the body until it finds a way out.

The eruption isn't the problem.
  The accumulation is.

The guilt that follows
  And then—almost immediately—the guilt.
  Because you erupted over nothing.
  Because they're just kids.
  Because you're supposed to be the adult.
  Because good mothers don't lose it over a dumb noise.
  But stay with me for a second:
  You didn't lose it over the noise.
  You lost it over everything that came before the noise that never got a moment to be acknowledged.
  The noise was just the messenger.
  Andddddd we shot the messenger.

Here's where it gets complicated—because the guilt isn't entirely wrong.
  The eruption probably wasn't your best moment. You know that. Pretending otherwise doesn't serve you or your kids.
  But there's a difference between guilt and shame that's worth under-standing:
  Guilt says - that didn't go the way I wanted.
  What would I do differently next time? What needs do I have that weren't met?

Shame says - I am the worst mother ever, I am fucking up my kids, I am bad for feeling angry at all.

Guilt is useful. It points somewhere. It asks good questions.

Shame just sits on you pointing it's accusatory finger and doesn't budge.

Put down the shame - it's not helpful.

Anger isn't the problem.

Anger is just information that arrived louder than you wanted it to.

You are not a bad mother because you have a breaking point.

You are a human being with a nervous system that finally said — enough.

The work isn't to never feel it.

The work is to catch it one moment earlier next time.

What the gift is actually telling you

When anger shows up—before you manage it, before you regulate it, before you breathe through it and make it smaller and more acceptable— ask it one question:

What boundary got crossed?

Not what triggered you.

What boundary.

Because anger doesn't show up randomly.

It shows up when something that matters to you has been violated—

your need for rest,

your need to be heard,

your need for reciprocity,

your need to exist as a person and not just a function

The anger is pointing at something real.

Listen to it before you extinguish it.

And then

After you've heard it - after you know what it's pointing at—then you figure out what to do with it.

You choose to respond instead of react.

You have the conversation when the timing is right and the little ears aren't listening.

But first—

Receive the gift.

Your anger is not your worst quality.

It's one of your most honest ones.

It knows where your edges are.

It knows what matters to you.

It knows when enough is enough before your conscious brain has caught up.

Honor that.

Activity

The next time you feel the volcano rising—before it erupts or right after—ask yourself one question:

What boundary just got crossed?

Not what annoyed you.

What boundary.

Write it down if you can.

Say it out loud if you can't.

Just name the real thing underneath the surface.

That's the gift.

53

9

Chapter 9: Hot Potato

Some feelings burn. And when they do, we don't hold them—we pass them.
Usually, to whoever made the unfortunate decision to stand closest to us
#hotpotato

Have you ever watched what happens when someone hears terrible news?

Not their reaction to it—what they do right after.

They find their person, and they tell them. All about the shitty, terrible, gut wrenching thing.

Not because that person can fix it.

Not because that person has the answers.

But because a feeling that size—sitting alone in your chest with nowhere to go—is

genuinely unbearable.

So we pass it.

Fast.

To whoever is the closest.

That's the hot potato.

Here's the thing about burning feelings — we are wired, deeply and biologically, to not hold them alone. Connection is how humans regulate. It's not weakness. It's neuroscience. When we're in distress, our nervous system actively seeks another nervous system to co-regulate with. We are literally built to find our people when things get hard.

The problem isn't that we pass the potato.

The problem is that we almost never stop to ask:

is this person actually equipped to hold this with me right now?

We just pass it. Fast. Because it's burning.

And what happens when you throw a burning potato at someone whose hands are already full of their own burning potatoes?

A few things can happen — none of them good.

Sometimes they catch it. Now they're burned too. Two people in pain, both raw, neither one equipped to help the other. What started as one person's hard feeling becomes a shared wound that somehow feels worse than the original.

Sometimes they drop it. The potato hits the floor and nobody knows whose it is anymore, and it burns a hole in the rug.

And sometimes — and this is the one that really gets us — they throw it back.

Hard.

Not because they're trying to hurt you. But because they're also burning. Because their hands were already full before you got there. Because an unprocessed feeling that lands on top of another unprocessed feeling doesn't create understanding — it creates an argument about who forgot to take out the trash six weeks ago.

You came in with a burning potato about feeling unseen. You left having a fight about the dishwasher.

Sound familiar?

That's not a communication failure. That's two nervous systems in distress colliding without a plan. The potato metaphor sounds silly — and it is — but the experience it describes is one of the most common and most painful dynamics in any close relationship.

The problem was never the potato.

The problem was never even the throwing.

The problem is that nobody stopped to ask — is this person actually in a position to catch this right now?

So what do we do instead?

The difference between witnessing and offloading

Here's the distinction that changed everything for me — and for a lot of the people I work with:

We don't actually need someone to take the feeling from us.

We need someone to sit next to us while we hold it ourselves.

That's the difference between being witnessed and offloading.

Offloading transfers the heat. It makes the other person responsible for your feelings — and now they're managing both their stuff and yours, and nobody is actually processing anything. You feel temporarily relieved. They feel suddenly burdened. And the feeling didn't go anywhere. It just changed hands.

Being witnessed is completely different.

It's someone saying — *I see you in this. I'm not going anywhere. You don't have to hold this alone, even though you're the one holding it.*

That's it. That's all it takes.

And here's the most useful sentence I know for asking for what you actually need:

"I don't need you to fix this. I just need you to sit with me for a minute."

That one sentence has saved more conversations than any conflict resolution framework I've ever come across. Because it tells the other person exactly what role to play — and it's a role most people can actually manage.

Who you hand it to matters

Not everyone is equipped to witness.

Not because they don't love you — but because they're human. They have their own potatoes. And some people were never taught how to hold space for someone else's fire without trying to extinguish it, catch it, or somehow make it about themselves.

Know your people. Know who can hold it and who will just get burned and burn you back.

And if there's no one available right now — and sometimes there genuinely isn't — find a safe container for the feeling until there is. Write it down. Take a shower. Take a walk. Let it exist somewhere outside your body without throwing it at someone who can't catch it.

The feeling will still be there when the right person is available.

Feelings are patient like that.

When the timing is just wrong

Our bodies are such tattletales.

If you're feeling off, people around you will sense it — even if they can't name it.

And more often than not you'll be asked the worst question in the English language:

"What's wrong?"

To which most people say "nothing" — which immediately and obviously indicates that something is very, very wrong.

If the moment isn't right — little ears listening, overtired before bed, about to walk into your in-laws' Friday dinner — try this instead:

"You're perceptive. Something is wrong, but this isn't the right time."

That one sentence does everything. It honors the feeling. It protects the moment. And it buys you the time you need to actually figure out what you want to say before you say it.

Because sometimes the most emotionally intelligent thing you can do is wait.

On never going to sleep angry

For the first three years of my marriage, I followed this advice religiously.

I kept us up until the wee hours of the morning, absolutely committed to resolving everything before we closed our eyes. I can tell you with complete certainty that nothing good came from those nights. Nothing got resolved. We were both exhausted. And in the morning the gut-wrenching feeling was still exactly where we left it — except now we were also sleep-deprived and slightly unhinged.

Some feelings need sleep more than they need resolution.

Some conversations need a rested brain and a regulated nervous system — not two people running on fumes at 2am trying to be emotionally mature.

You can go to sleep.

The feeling will wait.

You'll handle it better in the morning.

It took me a long time to realize that not all advice actually works for me in real life.

This was one of them.

Along with things like how often couples should be having sex, the idea that everything needs to dealt with immediately, or that a good mother never loses her patience.

None of that is true for everyone all the time.
And trying to uphold these truths for me at least was just another way I felt like I was failing at humaning.

Activity
Next time you feel the potato burning — before you pass it — ask yourself two questions:

What do I actually need right now — witnessing or fixing?
And is the person I'm about to hand this to actually equipped to give me that?

If the answer to the second question is no — find your safe container first.
They deserve the version of you that's already done the first round of holding.

10

Chapter 10: It's Not Just the Dishes - The Need to Be Seen

"I don't want to be appreciated. I want the dishwasher emptied
before I ask."
#DontMakeEyeContact

Being seen doesn't feel the way you think it does.

It doesn't arrive as a grand gesture. It doesn't show up in a perfectly timed conversation where someone finally says the exact right thing and you feel understood at a cellular level.

It feels like walking into the kitchen and the dishwasher is already empty.

It feels like the laundry that moved itself from the washer to the dryer while you were doing seventeen other things. The trash that disappeared before it started filing its own taxes. The dinner that someone else decided, planned, and executed without a single question directed at you.

It feels like not having to ask.

That's it. That's the whole thing.

Not love. Not appreciation. Not a heartfelt conversation about how much you do.

Just someone seeing the thing before you had to point at it.

Because the pointing — the noticing, the assessing, the delegating, the following up — that's the invisible work. That's the part that costs you. And when someone does it without being asked, even once, even for something small — you feel it in your chest like a door opening.

That's what being seen actually feels like.

Nobody reminds you

Nobody reminds me to buy the groceries.

Nobody sets an alarm for me to make dinner—dinner that needs to feed five people, not just myself.

Nobody checks whether the clothes needed for the week have been washed.

Nobody notices the dishes in the sink until I've already noticed them, assessed them, and either done them or added them to the running list in my head that never fully clears.

Imagine if they did.

Hey—don't forget to feed everyone tonight. Hey—the laundry. Hey— groceries.

The absurdity of that image is exactly my point.

You don't need reminding.

You don't forget.

You can't forget.

The list lives in you permanently—running quietly in the background of every moment of your day whether you want it to or not.

Nobody holds the map but you.

And here's what makes it invisible:

Everyone benefits from the map.

They just don't know it exists.

The ostrich

My favorite of the archetypes is the ostrich.

Not because they're easy to live with.

But because they're impossible to stay mad at—and that might be the most maddening thing about them.

There's a particular kind of partner (or child, or family member) who is not cruel.

Not lazy.

Not aggressive.

Not resistant.

They're not withholding.

They're not making a statement.

They're just conveniently... not looking.

You know that thing dogs do when they've eaten something they weren't supposed to? They won't look at you. Full body avoidance. Suddenly very interested in the corner of the room.

Kids do it too. You walk in, something is clearly wrong, and they are staring at literally anything that isn't your face.

The ostrich has mastered this energy.

Not guilty exactly.

Just... conveniently unaware.

Deeply committed to not making eye contact.

Head in the sand.

Peaceful.

Unbothered.

Completely unaware that the cat is hungry, the dishwasher is full, the laundry has been sitting in the dryer since Tuesday, and dinner isn't going to make itself for five people.

And here's the thing about the ostrich—
They are genuinely available.
Willing—once directed.
Helpful—once asked.
Present—once summoned.

Apologetic when it's pointed out.
"Oh, sorry. Of course I'll help."

And they mean it.
Every single time.
There is no malice.
No eye roll.
No reluctance.

They show up, do the thing, and feel genuinely good about themselves for helping.

And you stand there watching them feed the cat—the cat you noticed was hungry twenty minutes ago, the cat you assessed needed feeding, the cat you decided someone else should feed, the cat you had to formulate a request around and deliver at the right moment so it would actually land, the cat we rescued for *you* —and you think:

You just did one step.
I did five.
And you feel great.

And I feel invisible.

That's the ostrich.
  Not the villain of the story.
  Just the one who only sees the last step and mistakes it for the whole thing.
  And the having to ask—that's the part that makes you disappear.
  Because the asking means you saw it first.
  Again.
  You always see it first.
  And nobody ever sees you seeing it.
  The need to be seen

There's no shame in wanting to feel seen.
  Heard.
  Understood.
  Acknowledged.

It's one of the most fundamental human needs there is.
  We are wired for it.
  We suffer without it.

The problem isn't the need.
  The problem is when we keep seeking it from people who aren't equipped to provide it.
  The ostrich who genuinely doesn't see.
  The partner who is underwater in their own load.
  The friend who listens but always redirects to herself.
  Seeking visibility from someone who can't see you doesn't make you seen.
  It just makes you more exhausted.

So before you have the conversation—the one where you explain again what you need, again, and why it matters, again—ask yourself one thing:

Is this person actually capable of seeing me in the way I need right now?

Not do they love you.

Not are they a good person.

Are they capable of this specific thing in this specific moment?

Because you cannot explain yourself into being seen by someone who isn't looking.

Validate the shit out of yourself.

Not as a consolation prize.

As a foundation.

Start here — even if it's just in your own head:

I did that. I noticed. I held the map today and nobody saw it and it still got done.

That counts.

The more solid your own sense of being seen—by yourself, for yourself— the less desperate the seeking becomes. And the less desperate the seeking, the more clearly you can identify who actually *can* see you—and let them in.

Activity

Two questions. Just sit with them.

Who in your life actually sees you—not the role, not the function, not the mother and the manager and the one who holds the map—but you?

If someone comes to mind — when did you last let them in

If nobody comes to mind — that's not a failure.

That's information.

And it might be the most important thing this chapter helped you notice.

III

PART III: Becoming

Own Your Shit Into Empowerment

Chapter 11: Put Yourself in Time Out

"If I ever go missing, follow my kids. They can find me no matter where I try to hide." #TimeOut

There are moments in motherhood where you are one comment, one noise, one tiny human request away from completely losing your shit.

Not because you're a bad mother.

Because you're a full one.

Full of noise.

Full of decisions.

Full of being needed every single second of every single day - by people who love you completely and have absolutely no idea what that costs.

And the expectation—the unspoken one that nobody put in writing but somehow everyone absorbed - is that you just keep going.

Push through.

Stay calm.

Be patient.

Be present.

Always be better.

But here's the thing nobody really says out loud:

Sometimes the most responsible thing you can do as a mother is remove yourself.

Not forever.

Not dramatically.

Not in a way that requires explanation or apology or a family meeting.

Just briefly.

A timeout.

Not for your kids.

For you.

The slow-motion clusterfuck

Here's what I know about my own breaking point—I can see it coming.

It's like watching a scab you know you absolutely should not pick. You know it will bleed. You know it will scar. And yet it itches so badly that you cannot seem to stop yourself from going there anyway.

I watch the spiral start.

I see everything about to go sideways in slow motion.

And I stay anyway.

Watching.

Unable to step out of it.

We were flying back from Miami.

Full flight.

Overpacked row.

My seat area was a disaster—coloring books, snacks, water bottles, my youngest's entire portable world crammed into eighteen inches of airplane space.

I asked my eldest to pass me a few of her candies to give her little sister.
   "Just take the bag," she said.

I told her no—just hand me three, the bag won't fit.

And somewhere between her intention and execution, the bag slipped through her fingers—and half the contents scattered across the germ-infested airplane floor in a rainbow of tiny circular chaos.

I was immediately annoyed.

I whisper-scolded her.
   That specific kind of shouty-caps whisper that somehow feels worse than actual yelling because everyone around you can hear it but you're pretending they can't.

"Why couldn't you just hold the bag!"

She didn't mean to. It slipped. And my eldest, who, like most eldest kids have an aversion to making mistakes, immediately crumpled.

I knew that.

I watched myself in real time being unkind about something that was genuinely an accident.

And I did it anyway.

The woman in the seat next to us flinched. I saw her. I registered it. And yet I kept going.

My eldest felt terrible. And then my middle—her self-appointed protector since birth - immediately jumped in to take the blame. To absorb it. To redirect my annoyance onto himself so she wouldn't have to carry it.

Because that's who he is.

And there I was.

On my hands and knees on an airplane floor - germ-infested, deeply unglamorous, and straight up gross - picking up multicolored candies one by one.

My son beside me. Helping without even being asked. Because of course he was.

I knew better.

I teach this.

I help other people regulate their nervous systems for a living.
    And I still ended up on that floor. Super annoyed. A little ashamed. And very aware of the woman who totally heard the entire debacle and flinched.

The pause that changes everything
    This chapter isn't for the mothers who don't know better.
    It's for the ones who do—and still can't always stop themselves.
    Because knowing and doing are two completely different things.
    Especially when you're full.

Especially when you're tired.

Especially when you're in a confined space and everyone needs something and the candies are on the floor.

The pause—the timeout—isn't a cure.

It's a practice.

It's catching it one moment earlier than yesterday.

Not perfectly.

Not every time.

Just one moment earlier.

You've already felt this moment.

The rise.

The tight chest.

The noise getting louder—even when it isn't.

That version of you that is starting to surface —the one you don't actually want running the show.

That's your cue.

Not to try harder.

To pause.

Go to the bathroom.

Step outside.

Stand at the sink.

Drink water.

Breathe like a human being for thirty seconds.

You are not abandoning your kids.

You are regulating yourself.

And a regulated mother is a safer, more present, more honest mother than one who stayed and exploded.

We're so quick to send our kids to regulate.

"Go take a minute."
"Take a breath."
"Reset."
But we don't give ourselves that same permission.
Instead we stay.
We push.
We snap.
And then we sit in the guilt afterward.
What if the pause came before the snap?
What if instead of powering through—you stepped away?

Not as failure.

As awareness.
That's it.
That's the work.

You have permission to leave the room.

12

Chapter 12: Boundaries - My Late-Blooming Superpower

"I thought I had boundaries. Turns out I just had expectations that nobody else knew existed." #Whycantyoureadmymind

I assumed people would just *know*—what I needed, what I meant, where my limits were.

And when they didn't, I didn't speak up.

I just got quieter.

Tighter.

And eventually... resentful.

For a long time, I thought boundaries were about other people.

What they should do.

What they shouldn't do.

How they should show up.

I thought if I was clear enough, good enough, patient enough—people would just meet me there.

They didn't.

Not because they didn't care.

Because they didn't know.

And underneath all of it—every moment of frustration, every buildup of resentment, every quiet internal "are you kidding me?"—was something deeper:

A boundary that was never set.

Or one that was set... and never held.

That was the part I didn't understand for a long time.

Boundaries aren't about controlling other people.

They're about taking responsibility for what you allow, what you participate in, and what you continue to show up for.

And that's uncomfortable.

Because it means you don't get to sit in blame.

You have to look at your part.

Anger taught me that.

Not because anger is the problem.

But because anger is the signal.

It shows up when something matters.

When something is off.

When something has gone unspoken for too long.

The problem isn't that you're angry.

The problem is that you've been overriding yourself for so long that anger is the only voice left loud enough to get your attention.

And once you start listening—really listening—you begin to see it everywhere.

The moments you say yes when you mean no.

The times you step in when you didn't have to.

The situations you stay in longer than you should.
Not because you want to.
Because you haven't given yourself permission not to.

That's what boundaries actually are.

Permission.
Permission to say no.
Permission to disappoint someone.
Permission to choose yourself without needing a full explanation.

And here's the part that took me the longest to understand:

Setting a boundary doesn't mean the other person will like it.
They might not.
They might push back.
They might not understand.
They might even be upset.
That doesn't mean the boundary is wrong.
It means it's new.

You're not responsible for how other people feel about your boundaries.
You're responsible for whether you honor them.

Because every time you don't—you teach yourself that your needs are negotiable.

And every time you do— even when it's uncomfortable, even when your voice shakes, even when it would be easier to just go along with it—you reinforce something deeper:

I matter too.

Not more than everyone else.
But not less either.

You have permission to disappoint someone.

13

Chapter 13: What Even Is Grace? And How Are We Supposed to Embody It?

"Sure, sometimes I question my parenting. But to be honest, sometimes I question my child's childing." #GraceYourself

Grace.

It's one of those words that sounds soft and spiritual and slightly out of reach—like something you're supposed to have figured out by now, but somehow haven't.

Here's what I actually think it means:

The permission to expand when you inhale.

And—if you're courageous—to exhale audibly, even if you annoy everyone around you.

That's it.

Not a virtue.

Not something you earn.

Just a little more room.

A little less rigidity.

The space between who you think you're supposed to be—and who you actually are on

a Tuesday at 7 p.m. when everyone is losing their minds and you haven't eaten all day.

What gets in the way

Thinking.

Perfectionism.

Unattainable standards.

And one very specific voice in your head who has opinions about all of it. Constantly. Without being asked.

I call her the inner bitch.

She has different names depending on who she's visiting. I've met Beth. Mandy. Quintella. Bob. She shows up in different outfits for different people—corporate, maternal, occasionally disguised as your conscience, but she always says some version of the same thing:

You're fucking it all up.

Your kids. Your household. Your priorities are not in the right alignment. Why do you look like that?

Sound familiar?

She is relentless. She is specific. She knows exactly which tender spot to press and she presses it at the worst possible moment — usually when you're already tired, already stretched, already doing your absolute best with what you have.

And here's the thing most people don't realize about her:

She is not trying to destroy you.

She genuinely thinks she's helping.

What actually works

Most people want to silence her. Push her out. Pretend she's not there. That doesn't work. Trust me –I've tried.

What does work?

Thank her.
Not sarcastically.
Not through gritted teeth.
Genuinely.

Because she's not evil. She was built to protect you—to keep you on track, push you to do better, keep you safe from failure and judgment and falling short. She's been doing this job for years. Decades maybe. She just never got the memo that the threat level changed.
She's just running outdated software.
She thinks harsh criticism equals high standards. She thinks if she lets up for even a second you'll stop trying altogether. She thinks the only way to keep you safe is to make sure you never feel too comfortable, too confident, too settled.
She's wrong. But she means well.

Separate the voice
Give her a name.
Something that makes her feel separate from you. Because she is not you.
She's just a voice that got loud and comfortable living rent-free in your head.

Here's why the name matters — you can't argue with a feeling. You can't reason with a fog. But you can absolutely tell Beth to sit the fuck down.

The moment you name her, she stops being you and starts being something you can have a relationship with. Something that doesn't automatically get to be in charge just because it showed up.

My son's inner critic is named Bob. When Bob shows up and tells him he's bad at soccer, basketball, baseball (basically any team competitive sport) — He now knows it's Bob talking. Not truth. Not fact. Bob.

Name her. See her. And then say:

Thanks for stopping by. I've got it from here.

That gap — between her voice and your response — is where you get your power back.

Not in silencing her. Not in being perfect. Just in remembering that you get to decide what you do with what she says.

The filter

The thing about that voice is that sometimes — annoyingly — she holds a sliver of truth.

Not the cruel version she's delivering.

Not *you're terrible at this,* or *you'll never figure it out,* or *nobody could love someone like you.*

But underneath the cruelty? Sometimes there's something worth hearing.

Maybe it's not that *you're a bad athlete* — maybe you've been holding back and you know it. Maybe it's not that *you're a terrible cook* — maybe meal planning would actually change your life and you've been avoiding it.

Maybe it's not that *you'll never find love* — maybe you haven't learned to enjoy your own company yet and that's worth sitting with.

The filter isn't about dismissing everything she says. It's about separating the message from the method.

Is it true? Is it kind? And what I recite to my kids daily —

"if it's not true and it's not kind it has no space in your mind" - the rhyme just helps it stick.

If it's not true and it's not kind — out.

If there's truth in it but it's not kind — that's the one worth looking at.

Gently.

On your own terms.

Not hers.

Not Gunna Name Any Names - Everett

My son came home one day and told me a kid from his class said he was weird. This wasn't the first time, this kid has gotten under his skin a few times. He'd critiqued his athletic abilities. He'd talk smack about him to other kids behind his back - except it was kind of in front of his face, he just didn't see him standing there. And now this. Straight up calling him weird.

My first thought?

Fuck that kid.

I wanted to tell my son to fire back — that bruh looks like he belongs in second grade and walks around like he's permanently sucking on a lemon.

Not my proudest moment.

But let's be real — the mama bear doesn't consult her framework first. She just shows up. Claws out.

Then I remembered I'm supposed to be a somewhat functioning adult.

So I took a breath and said:

"Listen. We're all a little weird. So maybe you are a little weird. But is it

kind? No. So it doesn't get to hold space in your mind."

Run it through the filter.

Is it true? Maybe — we're all a little weird.

Is it kind? Absolutely not.

So we don't keep it. We don't let nonsense live rent-free in our heads.

Use it on yourself

This works for your inner voice too.

And this is where it gets a little more complicated - because unlike Everett, your inner voice sometimes has a point.

"You're a terrible mother." Is it true? No. Is it kind? No. Out - immediately no discussion.

"I lost my patience today." Is it true? Maybe. Is it kind? Not super. So we adjust:

"I lost my patience today. I was tired and full and I'm human. Tomorrow I will try again. What do I need so tomorrow looks different?"

You're not letting yourself off the hook.

You're just refusing to let the criticism be crueler than it needs to be.

And sometimes — when you actually get quiet enough to listen underneath the noise — you realize what she's really trying to say isn't *you're terrible.*

It's something much simpler. My inner bitch typically means
You're not present. You're not in the moment. You're not having fun.

And the answer to that isn't a framework.

It's simpler than anything I could teach you.

What she is saying to me is go spend fun time with your kids.

Not perfectly. Not with a plan. Not because you've earned it or figured it out or finally got everything right.

Just show up. Be there. Let that be enough.

That's grace.

Activity

Name her.

The voice that shows up when you're in the thick of it—the one telling you you're failing, your priorities are off, you're not enough.

Give her a name.

Then ask:

What are you trying to protect me from?

And is there a kinder way to do it?

Because she's not wrong that something needs attention.

She's just being mean about it.

You have permission to exhale ... loudly.

14

Chapter 14: You Can Do Hard Things

"Sometimes the hardest thing a person can do is nothing at all."
#SittingStill

The front seat

My daughter was in fourth grade.

We have a big group of friends—a real community. The kind of community people spend their whole lives looking for. Among the kids, there are eight girls who are around the same age and have formed a truly unique group.

And like any group of kids growing up - there were seasons where social dynamics were hard to navigate.

My daughter is a little different. She moves to the beat of her own drum. A little evasive. Not a fan of confrontation. I have always quietly admired her for it even when it worried me a bit. Social groups can be complicated - not because anything is wrong with them, or the other kids, but because navigating situations is tricky as an adult, how could it not be even trickier as a child.

Like most children at one point or another in adolescence there were feelings of being left out—and for my daughter specifically it was around sleepovers.

One particular night, she got invited to a sleepover.

I was out at dinner with the other moms.

Mid-dinner, the hosting mom got a call—her daughter had a stom-achache, wasn't feeling well - and she asked if my daughter could go home early and not spend the night.

At the same time, I got a call from my daughter asking if I could pick her up.

Of course.

No problem.

I was the driver, so I took the other moms home first.

When I pulled up, my daughter was already waiting on the steps—duffle bag in hand, silent.

An unreadable mask on her face.

A kind smile as she waved goodbye.

But I know that face.

It looks exactly like mine.

The one I use when I don't feel safe enough to experience my feelings.

She was silent the entire ride.

I said nothing.

There was another mom in the car, and I was hyper-aware of the strength it was taking for my little girl to hold it together.

I could feel it from the front seat.

I knew exactly what was happening.

And I said nothing.

I dropped the last mom off.

And my daughter moved to the front seat.

And she fell apart.

She cried the way you cry when something hits a part of you that was already tender.

The rejection.

The exclusion.

The not being chosen—again—by the girls who were seemed to be always choosing each other.

I held her.

I didn't tell her it wasn't what she thought.

I didn't say the friend really was sick.

I didn't reframe it or minimize it or offer tools.

I just held her and let her feel it.

In all her years, I had never seen her hurt like that.

And in all my years of motherhood, I'm not sure I've ever done anything harder than sitting in that front seat, feeling everything she felt, and choosing not to fix it. In that moment it wasn't about explaining the situation or easing her feelings, it was about allowing her to feel them fully and letting her know she was safe to do so.

The hardest thing

Not the sleepless nights.

Not the witching hour.

Not the mental load.

This.

Witnessing your child's pain without trying to stop it.

Because everything in you wants to make it better.

The urge is physical—almost unbearable.

You are wired to protect them.

To fix it.

To say the thing that makes the hurt smaller.

To reframe.

And sometimes the most loving thing you can do...is *to don't*. Don't do.

Sometimes the most loving thing is just:

Presence.
Stillness.
Your arms.
Your silence.
A front seat and enough space for her to fall apart while you hold it all without flinching.
That's not passive.
That's the most active thing I know how to do.
To stay.
To witness.
To not make her pain about my discomfort with her pain.
Feelings that are witnessed move through.
Feelings that are fixed or minimized just go underground and wait.

You've already done it
You've already done the hard thing.
Probably today.
Maybe an hour ago.
Not perfectly.
Not gracefully.
But you stayed.
You witnessed.
You held space for something that was almost unbearable to hold.
And you didn't make it about you.

That counts.

Even if no one saw it.
Even if no one acknowledged it.
Even if it didn't look the way you thought strength was supposed to look.

You did it.
And you'll do it again.
Not because it's easy.
Because you can.

You have permission to witness without fixing.

15

Chapter 15: The Magical Ordinary

"I used to think there would be a moment I'd have it all figured out. Turns out that's not how any of this works"
#TheMagicalOrdinary

I used to think there would be a moment where everything clicked.
Where I felt fully like myself again.
Where motherhood felt balanced.
Where the chaos settled and something clear and calm took its place.
That moment never came.

Instead, something quieter happened.
Nothing changed—and everything did.
The kids still need things.
The noise is still there.
The mental load didn't magically disappear.
But I'm different inside it.

I still get overwhelmed.

I still lose my patience.
I still have days where it all feels like too much.
But I don't spiral the same way anymore.

Less resistant.
Less reactive.
Less convinced that I'm doing it wrong.

More aware.
More honest.
More willing to let things be what they are.

There is no version of this where everything is handled perfectly.
There is just this version.
The ordinary one.
The one where you're still figuring it out.
Still getting it wrong sometimes.
Still learning how to hold yourself and everyone else at the same time.

And somehow—inside all of that—there are moments.
Small ones.

A walk.
A laugh.
Sitting in the car for one extra minute before going inside.
A breath where nothing is being asked of you.

That's it.
That's the magic.

Not in fixing everything.

Not in becoming someone else.

In noticing what's already here.

You didn't go back to who you were.
    You became someone else entirely.
    And she's still unfolding.

You have permission to let this be enough.

16

Conclusion

You're Not Alone in the Cracks
You made it to the end.
Not because everything is fixed.
Not because you have the answers.
Not because motherhood suddenly makes sense.
But because something in these pages felt true.
And you kept going.

That's not nothing.
That's everything.

So before you close this book, just remember:
The cracks you've been living in—the ones that feel like failure, like fracture, like proof that you're doing it wrong—
They were never just yours.
Every mother reading this has her own version of the witching hour.
Her own airplane floor.
Her own front seat in the dark.
Her own inner bitch with a name.

Her own version of the woman on the porch she's always chasing.

We are all in the cracks.

And the cracks—as it turns out—are exactly where the light gets in.

You didn't finish this book and become a different person.

You finished it and remembered who you already were.

Underneath the noise.

Underneath the mental load.

Underneath the having to ask, the holding it together, the showing up even when there was nothing left to show up with.

She was always there.

Still unfolding.

Still becoming.

Still worthy of being seen.

A note about what comes next

I've been thinking about community.

Not a perfect one.

Not a curated one.

Not an Instagram version of motherhood where everyone looks like they have it together.

A real one.

A place where the inner bitch has a name.

Where the witching hour is understood.

Where nobody has to explain why they cried in the car, or ate the Trader Joe's mini-Snickers without sharing, or let the TV babysit for twenty minutes just to breathe.

A place where being a grain of sand on a beach full of them—honest, imperfect, still figuring it out—is exactly enough.

A place between the cracks.

I'm thinking of building it.

And if you want in, join it.

And if you just want to talk one-on-one—email me:
orlikoshet@gmail.com
I actually read them.

Let's find the light.

Go get some glasses. It's about to get a whole lot brighter.

About the Author

Orli Koshet holds a PhD exploring motherhood, confidence, and the way women build self-efficacy.

She works with women navigating the emotional weight of motherhood, relationships, and identity — helping them make sense of what feels overwhelming, unspoken, or just hard to name.

This book came from real life — the messy, the hard, and the moments that don't get said out loud enough. She's still figuring it out. Like most of us.